DRAW FANTASY CREATURES

BY A.J. SAUTTER

48 CREATURE PROJECTS

CAPSTONE PRESS
a capstone imprint

TABLE OF CONTENTS

BRING YOUR IMAGINATION TO LIFE!

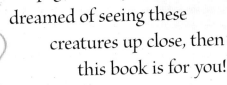

Have you ever imagined meeting a magical elf or dwarf in an enchanted forest? How would you like to test your strength against a deadly fire-breathing dragon or a horde of wicked orcs? Do you long to ride into unknown adventures on a griffin or pegasus? If you've ever dreamed of seeing these creatures up close, then this book is for you!

Fantastic creatures such as these may only exist in books and films. But they often thrive in our imaginations. You won't be facing any goblins, harpies, or centaurs in real life. But you can bring these and other fantasy creatures to life by drawing them. Grab some paper and pencils and prepare to set your imagination loose.

Just follow the drawing steps in each project to begin sketching trolls, elves, boggarts, and many other incredible creatures. Once you've mastered drawing them, you can try drawing them in new poses, settings, or situations. You can even try creating scenes showing your favorite creatures battling each other in amazing fantasy worlds. When your art is ready, you can breathe life into it by coloring it with colored pencils, markers, or paint. Are you ready to set your inner artist free? Let's get started!

FINDING YOUR STYLE

Don't worry if your art isn't exactly like the drawings you see in this book. As you'll see, artists use a wide range of styles. If you keep practicing, your own art style will develop over time. Soon you'll be creating awesome creatures and fantasy artwork of your very own.

GATHER YOUR SUPPLIES

Before you start drawing, you'll need to gather some basic supplies. With paper, pencils, erasers, and sharpeners in hand, you'll be ready to sketch anything your imagination can create.

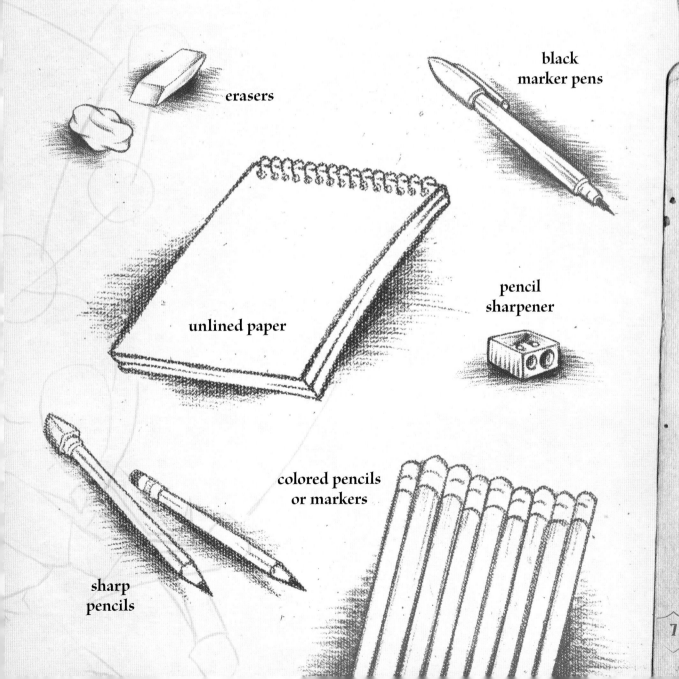

erasers

black marker pens

unlined paper

pencil sharpener

colored pencils or markers

sharp pencils

RED DRAGONS

Red dragons have terrible tempers. They'll attack anyone who intrudes on their territories. Red dragons are also extremely greedy. They guard their huge treasure hoards fiercely. If even a single coin is stolen, they'll fly into a terrible rage and burn nearby farms and villages to the ground to find the thief.

SIZE: 150 FEET (46 METERS) LONG OR MORE; WINGSPANS UP TO 180 FEET (55 M)

HABITAT: LAIRS IN DEEP CAVES FOUND IN THE LARGEST MOUNTAIN RANGES

Physical Features: When these dragons hatch from their eggs, they're a bright shade of red. Their scales become dark red or red-gold as they age. Red dragons have razor-sharp claws and teeth, and powerful whiplike tails. Of course, red dragons are most famous for their fiery breath that is hot enough to melt steel.

1

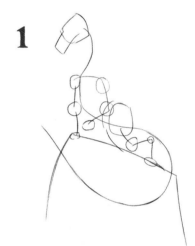

2

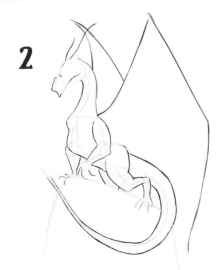

3

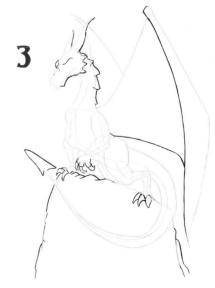

4

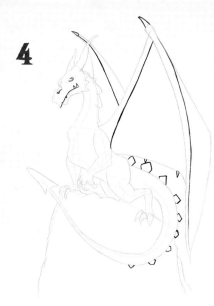

WHAT'S NEXT?

After practicing this dragon, try to draw it attacking a mountain village. Show it flying over and blasting the buildings with its fiery breath.

5

FINAL

6

WHITE DRAGONS

White dragons aren't as ferocious as red dragons or as cruel as black dragons. But they do have long memories. They've been known to seek revenge against those who insulted them many years before. Like most dragons, white dragons love treasure. But they especially enjoy glittering diamonds and silver coins.

SIZE: ABOUT 100 FEET (31 M) LONG; WINGSPANS UP TO 120 FEET (37 M)

HABITAT: LAIRS IN ICY CAVES FOUND ON MOUNTAIN PEAKS OR LARGE ICEBERGS

Physical Features: Young white dragons are very light in color. As they age their scales darken slightly or turn light blue. Unlike other dragons, white dragons have only two legs. But they do have wickedly sharp claws and teeth. White dragons also have an icy breath weapon that can freeze their enemies solid in an instant.

1

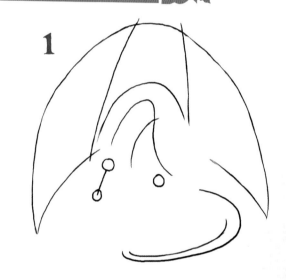

2

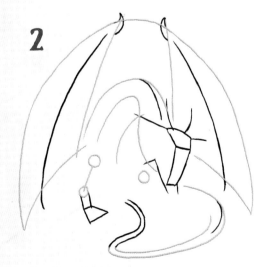

3

WHAT'S NEXT?

Next draw another white dragon hunting for its next meal. Show it using its icy breath to freeze its prey.

FINAL

4

5

BLACK DRAGONS

Black dragons are cruel and evil. They are known to enjoy hunting and killing other creatures simply to cause pain and suffering. Black dragons also love to hoard treasure. They tend to like gold coins more than gems or other valuable items.

SIZE: UP TO 120 FEET (37 M) LONG; WINGSPANS UP TO 150 FEET (46 M)

HABITAT: LAIRS IN HIDDEN CAVES OFTEN FOUND IN SWAMPS OR DARK JUNGLES

Physical Features:
Most black dragons have thin, bony bodies. Their skin often appears diseased. The thin skin on their wings tends to tear easily, so most don't fly well. Like most dragons, black dragons have deadly claws, teeth, and tails. Their hot acid breath weapon is strong enough to dissolve even the thickest of armor.

1

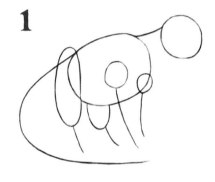

2

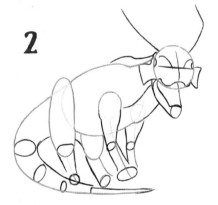

3

4

5

6

FINAL

WHAT'S NEXT?

Next try to draw this dragon inside its swampy lair as it guards its huge treasure of gold coins.

13

EASTERN DRAGONS

Eastern dragons are known for being wise and helpful toward humans. Eastern dragons are sometimes said to magically bring rain to help farmers' crops grow during a drought. Eastern dragons are not greedy for treasure like other dragons. But they do like colorful gems such as rubies and emeralds.

SIZE: MORE THAN 200 FEET (61 M) LONG

HABITAT: LAIRS IN HIDDEN CAVES NEAR RIVERS AND LAKES

Physical Features: Eastern dragons are usually brightly colored. They have camel-like heads, giant snakelike bodies, and eaglelike talons on their feet. Eastern dragons do not have a breath weapon. They also don't have wings. But they do have a magical ability to fly.

1

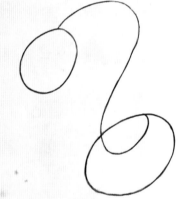

2

3

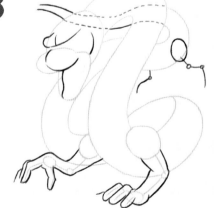

4

5

6

FINAL

WHAT'S NEXT?

After practicing the Eastern dragon, try drawing a scene showing it flying with a young person riding on its back.

MOUNTAIN GIANTS

Mountain giants like to live alone and can be dangerous when disturbed by outsiders. They often use huge, spiked clubs to smash enemies to the ground. Mountain giants sometimes engage in mock battles by hurling giant boulders at each other. After these battles, mountain valleys often look as if a large landslide has taken place.

SIZE: 45 FEET (14 M) TALL OR MORE

HABITAT: LARGE CAVES IN MOUNTAIN RANGES; SOME LARGE HOMES IN HIDDEN VALLEYS

Physical Features: Other than their enormous size, mountain giants look similar to humans. But their skin is thick and tough, and it is often a stonelike gray color. Mountain giants usually have black, brown, or fiery red hair. Most males also grow huge, bushy beards.

1

2

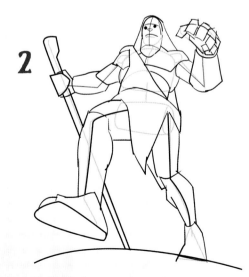

3

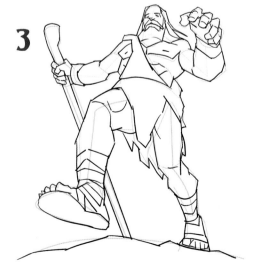

4

WHAT'S NEXT?

After drawing this huge giant, try drawing two of them throwing huge boulders at each other across a mountain valley.

FINAL

5

CYCLOPES

Cyclopes usually live alone and spend their days tending to their herds of animals. Many Cyclopes are also clever blacksmiths. They make high-quality weapons and armor. It's thought that some Cyclopes have created powerful magical items in their secret forges deep inside volcanoes.

SIZE: ABOUT 15 FEET (4.6 M) TALL

HABITAT: MOUNTAIN CAVES OR THE RUINS OF OLD STONE CASTLES

Physical Features: Cyclopes have stocky bodies and large, strong hands. They have tough skin that is often green or a stony gray color. Most Cyclopes don't have much hair, but a few may have thin beards. Cyclopes are best known for the single large eyes in the middle of their foreheads.

1

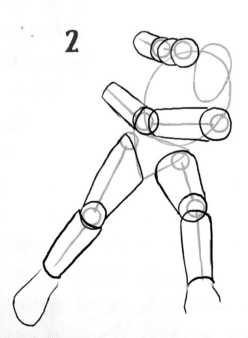

2

3

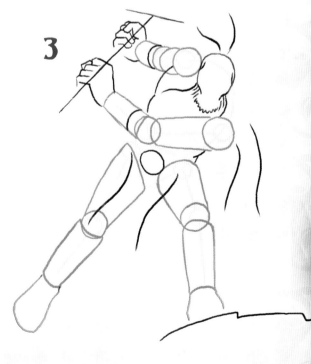

4

5

WHAT'S NEXT?

Next draw a Cyclops forging
a magical sword or shield.
Try to show it working in its
secret underground workshop.

FINAL

ETTINS

Ettins normally live alone in dark caves that stink of decaying food. They never bathe and are usually covered in layers of smelly dirt and grime. In spite of their multiple heads, ettins aren't very intelligent. However, they are skilled with multiple weapons in combat. Ettins are fierce fighters and will usually fight to the death.

SIZE: ABOUT 20 TO 25 FEET (6 TO 7.6 M) TALL

HABITAT: DARK UNDERGROUND CAVES IN REMOTE ROCKY REGIONS

Physical Features: Ettins have tall, muscular bodies with two or more heads. Each head controls a different part of the body. Their thick skin is tough and protects them as a natural form of armor. Their hair is often long and stringy and is usually black or dark brown. Some ettins may also grow thick, bushy beards.

2

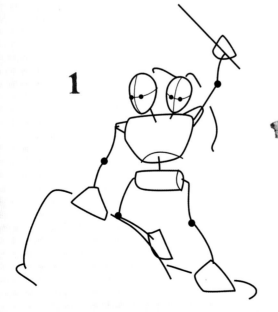

1

WHAT'S NEXT?

When you're finished drawing this ettin, try drawing him again as he battles against a nasty ogre or troll.

20

3

4

FINAL

5

OGRES

Ogres are naturally violent and cruel. They enjoy torturing enemies and love hearing them cry out in pain. Ogres aren't very intelligent and have few skills. They often go on night raids to steal food and other goods that they can't make themselves. Although sunlight doesn't harm ogres, they hate it and avoid it whenever possible.

SIZE: 8 TO 10 FEET (2.4 TO 3 M) TALL

HABITAT: DARK, DAMP CAVES IN FOOTHILLS NEAR MOUNTAINS; SOME LIVE NEAR STINKING BOGS OR SWAMPS

Physical Features: Ogres have incredibly strong and muscular bodies. They also have very tough skin, which is usually green or gray-green in color. Ogres also often have shortened legs, hunched backs, and other deformities. Many ogres have sharp tusks growing from their bottom jaws.

1

2

3

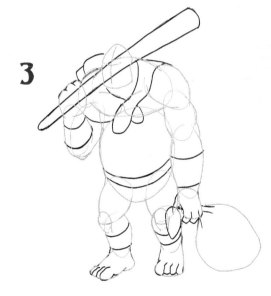

5

6

4

FINAL

WHAT'S NEXT?

Now try to draw a small group of ogres going on a nighttime raid at a local village. Show each ogre carrying a different kind of weapon to use in a fight.

CAVE TROLLS

Cave trolls are active only at night. If they're exposed to direct sunlight, their bodies turn to solid stone. Cave trolls spend most of their time looking for food and will often steal animals from nearby farms. Some cave trolls live with groups of orcs in the mountains. They'll fight alongside the orcs to ambush unsuspecting travelers in exchange for food.

SIZE: 10 TO 12 FEET (3 TO 3.7 M) TALL

HABITAT: DEEP, DARK CAVES IN HILLS AND MOUNTAIN REGIONS

Physical Features: Cave trolls are related to giants, which helps explain their huge size and strength. Cave trolls' tough skin strongly resembles rough stone. These dangerous creatures also have mouths filled with sharp jagged teeth and two large tusks.

1

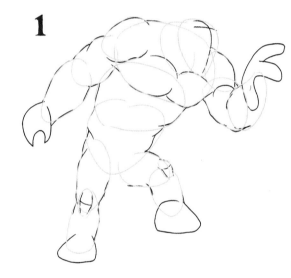

2

3

4

5

FINAL

WHAT'S NEXT?

Next try to draw this troll working with some orcs as they ambush a group of travelers in the mountains.

FOREST TROLLS

Forest trolls have rarely been seen. It's thought that they spend most of their time roaming the forest looking for food. A few forest trolls may wear armor and carry simple weapons. These trolls are known to attack intruders and will track down enemies through the thickest forests.

SIZE: 12 TO 15 FEET (3.7 TO 4.6 M) TALL

HABITAT: DARK CAVES FOUND IN THICK FORESTS IN NORTHERN REGIONS

Physical Features: Forest trolls are strong and muscular with long arms and short legs. They usually have gray or green-gray skin. But many are covered in coarse brown hair. Forest trolls have huge mouths filled with jagged, rotten teeth. They also have large tusks jutting out from their lower jaws.

1

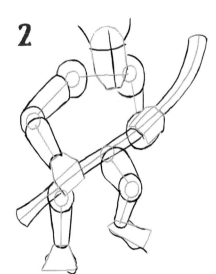

2

3

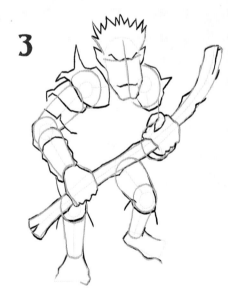

4

5

FINAL

WHAT'S NEXT?

After drawing this troll,
try drawing it chasing
some dwarves through
the thick forest.

SWAMP TROLLS

Swamp trolls are little more than savage beasts. They aren't intelligent, can't speak, and are very violent. They usually attack all living creatures on sight. Luckily, swamp trolls are sensitive to sunlight. They normally stay in their lairs during the day and are active only at night.

SIZE: 8 TO 10 FEET (2.4 TO 3 M) TALL

HABITAT: SWAMPS AND BOGS IN TROPICAL REGIONS

Physical Features: Swamp trolls aren't as large as other trolls, but they're incredibly strong. Their skin is usually dark green or black in color. Swamp trolls have strong hands tipped with wicked claws they use to slash at their prey. Swamp trolls heal quickly from wounds. They can also regrow lost arms or legs within minutes. Fire and acid are the only things that can destroy them.

1

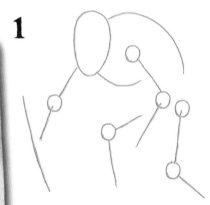

2

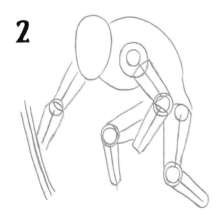

3

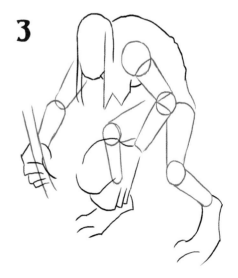

4

5

FINAL

WHAT'S NEXT?
Now try to draw a scene of another two swamp trolls fighting each other in a stinking swamp.

DRAGON vs. KNIGHT

Fantasy stories are filled with tales of brave knights battling huge, fire-breathing dragons. These armored warriors test their courage by attempting a deadly task that most people wouldn't dare to try. Many of these bold knights come to a fiery end in their quest. But those who succeed often find fame, fortune, and glory. Their daring deeds live forever in stories and songs.

DRAGON

SIZE: 150 FEET (46 METERS) LONG OR MORE; WINGSPANS UP TO 180 FEET (55 M)

HABITAT: DEEP CAVES FOUND IN THE LARGEST MOUNTAIN RANGES

KNIGHT

SIZE: 6 TO 6.5 FEET (1.8 TO 2 M) TALL

HOMES: STRONG CASTLES OR FORTRESSES MADE OF STONE

1

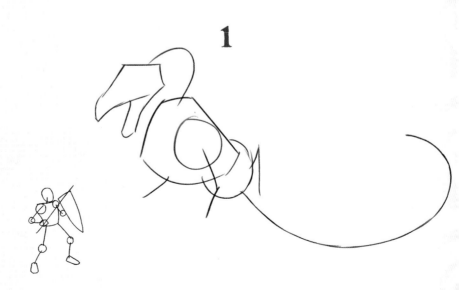

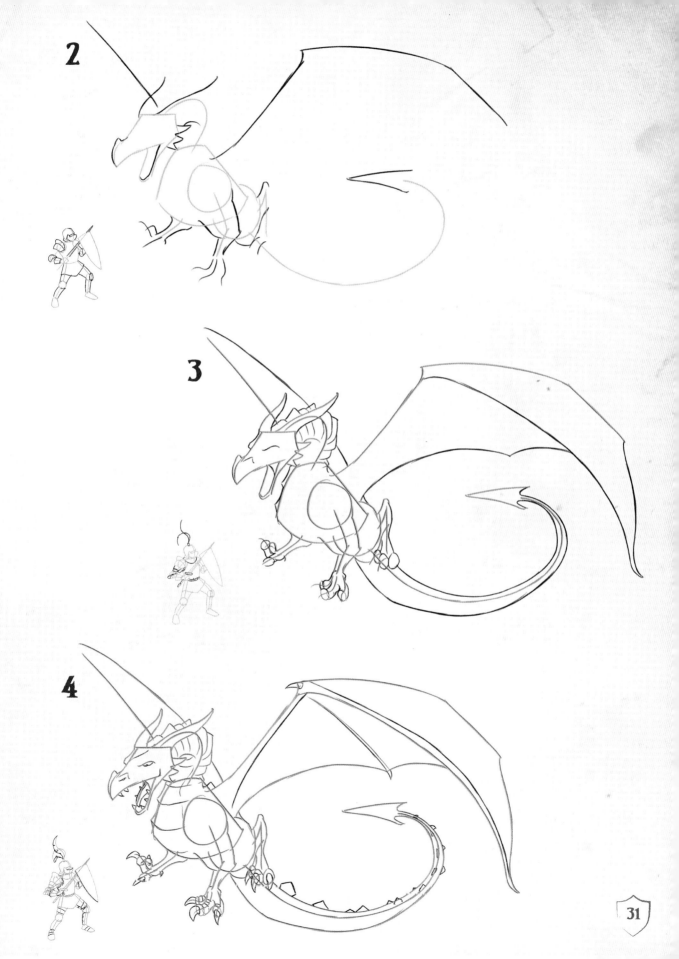

2

3

4

5

6

FINAL

WHAT'S NEXT?

After you've drawn this scene, try to draw what happens next. Is the knight successful in his quest to slay the dragon? Or is the dragon victorious over the brave but foolish armored warrior?

CENTAURS

Centaurs are proud creatures and normally keep to themselves. They rarely make friends with outsiders. However, centaurs are extremely loyal to the few friends they do have. They will gladly risk their lives to help friends in need. Centaurs are also very skilled with bows, swords, and other weapons and are deadly during a fight.

SIZE: ABOUT 7 TO 7.5 FEET (2.1 TO 2.3 M) TALL

HABITAT: FORESTS, PLAINS, AND FOOTHILLS NEAR MOUNTAINS

Physical Features: Centaurs are part human and part horse. Their human upper bodies are strong and muscular. They usually have long, flowing hair, and some males also grow bushy beards. Centaurs' powerful, horselike lower bodies are usually covered in dark brown or black hair.

1

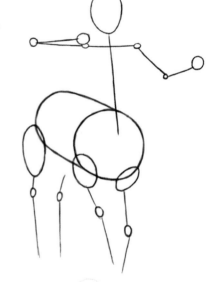

2

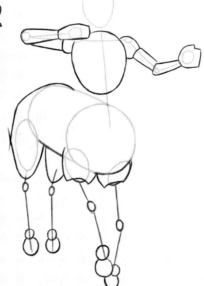

3

4

5

FINAL

WHAT'S NEXT?

When you've finished drawing this centaur, try drawing another rearing up on its hind legs or fighting an enemy with an axe.

SATYRS

Satyrs love a good party and having fun with their friends. They love nature and enjoy exploring forests. Most satyrs are also skilled musicians. They often play panpipes to cast magic musical spells to entertain their friends. Satyrs may also use their musical spells to confuse enemies or put them to sleep.

SIZE: ABOUT 5 TO 5.5 FEET (1.5 TO 1.7 M) TALL

HABITAT: THICK FORESTS AND HILLY REGIONS NEAR MOUNTAINS

Physical Features: Satyrs have legs and feet like goats and upper bodies similar to humans. Their heads and faces combine both human and goatlike features. They have long, narrow noses and large, curved horns. Many satyrs also have beardlike whiskers growing from their chins.

1

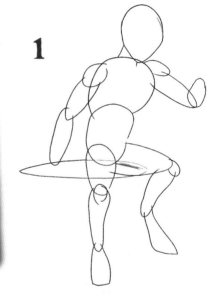

2

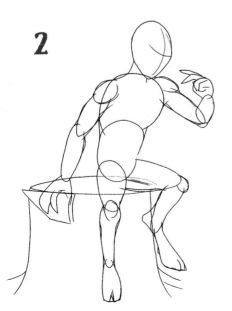

3

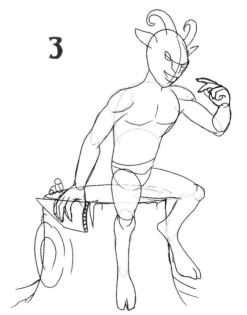

4

5

FINAL

WHAT'S NEXT?

Practice drawing this satyr a few
times. Then try drawing several
of them dancing and playing
music in a forest clearing.

FAIRIES

Fairies usually use their magical form to hide their true appearance. They are very curious and like to explore the world. Fairies are often friendly, talkative, and outgoing. However, they are easily angered by people who harm the natural world. They'll use their magic to scare off anyone they feel is a threat.

SIZE: IN MAGICAL FORM: THE SIZE OF LARGE BUTTERFLIES OR OTHER WINGED INSECTS

HABITAT: WOODLAND AREAS FILLED WITH STREAMS AND MEADOWS

Physical Features: In magical form fairies appear as butterflies, moths, dragonflies, and other flying insects. But in their true form they appear as beautiful young women. Fairies are best known for their large, lightweight wings attached to their backs.

1

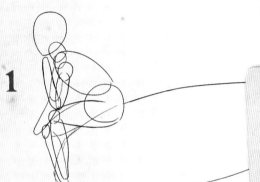

2

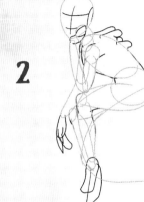

3

4

5

FINAL

WHAT'S NEXT?

Now try drawing another fairy
flying by some flowers. Give
her some different clothing or
different colorful wings.

BROWNIES

Brownies like to stay hidden, but they are very friendly. They often do household chores during the night, such as mending clothes, cleaning dishes, and mopping floors. Brownies never expect any payment. But they can be easily insulted if someone criticizes their work. They may hide important items or make large messes to get back at those who offended them.

SIZE: ABOUT 8 TO 12 INCHES (20 TO 30 CENTIMETERS) TALL

HABITAT: CRAWL SPACES, ATTICS, AND OTHER SMALL SPACES IN BARNS AND FARMHOUSES

Physical Features: Brownies are short creatures that appear somewhat ratlike. They have beady black eyes, pointed ears and noses, whiskers, and strong front teeth. Brownies usually wear shabby clothes made from scraps of cloth that they find while doing their work.

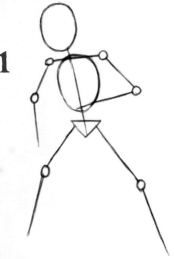

1

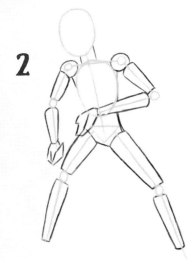

2

3

4

5

FINAL

WHAT'S NEXT?

After drawing this brownie, try drawing him in his living space with buttons, pins, and other small items he's collected.

GNOMES

Gnomes often seem gruff and unfriendly toward strangers. But they usually mean no harm. They simply prefer a peaceful life and little contact with outsiders. Gnomes spend most of their time gathering food or mining for gems underground. They are also skilled craftsmen. Their jewelry is often considered some of the finest in the world.

SIZE: ABOUT 18 TO 24 INCHES (46 TO 61 CM) TALL

HABITAT: SMALL CAVES AND HOLLOW TREES IN HILLY, WOODED AREAS

Physical Features: Gnomes are often mistaken for dwarves. However, gnomes have shorter legs and stockier bodies. They also have strong hands that are often scarred from working in their mines and workshops. Adult male gnomes usually have long white or gray beards.

1

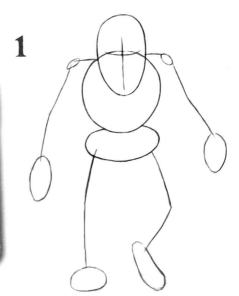

2

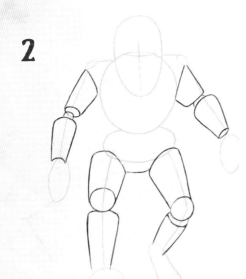

3

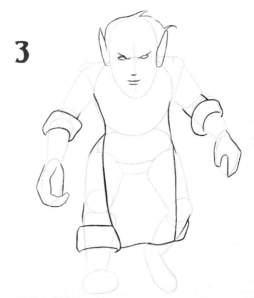

4

5

6

FINAL

WHAT'S NEXT?

After drawing this gnome, try a new drawing that shows him mining for gems or crafting a fine piece of jewelry.

HALFLINGS

Halflings are peaceful people who prefer a quiet life, good food, and the comforts of home. But in spite of their easygoing lifestyle, halflings can be tough. They can overcome many hardships when necessary. Halflings are also very stealthy and can move in total silence to avoid being seen by others.

SIZE: 3 TO 3.5 FEET (0.9 TO 1 M) TALL

HABITAT: DRY AND COMFORTABLE UNDERGROUND HOLES OR SMALL HOMES NEAR LAKES OR RIVERS

Physical Features: Halflings are about half the size of humans. Almost all halflings have curly brown hair. Male halflings sometimes grow bushy sideburns that frame their round faces. All halflings have large, tough feet covered in furry brown hair. They never wear shoes or boots.

1

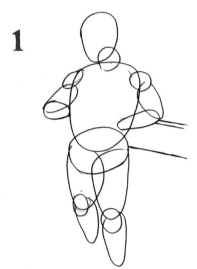

2

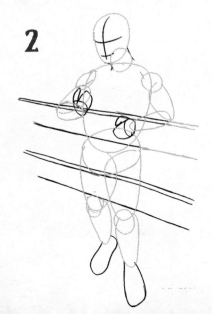

3

4

FINAL

5

6

WHAT'S NEXT?

Next try to draw another halfling as he tries to sneak past a hungry troll or a goblin hunting party.

DWARVES

Dwarves are expert miners and craftsmen. Few people can match the quality of their weapons, armor, and jewelry. A few dwarves are also skilled at creating powerful magical weapons and armor. Dwarves are a proud and noble people, but they are fiercely private. They don't like answering questions about their families. If offended, they'll simply turn and walk away.

SIZE: ABOUT 4 TO 4.5 FEET (1.2 TO 1.4 M) TALL

HABITAT: AMAZING CITIES BUILT INSIDE HUGE MOUNTAIN CAVES

Physical Features:
Dwarves are short but have strong, thickly muscled bodies. They often have lumpy ears and noses. Dwarf men take great pride in their long beards, which they often weave and braid into fantastic designs.

1

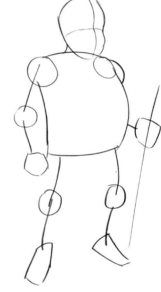

2

3

4

5

6

FINAL

WHAT'S NEXT?

Next try drawing a group of dwarves as they mine for gold and gems deep inside a mountain. Or try drawing a dwarf fighting a goblin or other enemy.

ELVES

Elves are peaceful people with great respect for nature. They also enjoy creating poetry, music, and fine crafts. But when necessary, elves can be fearsome warriors. Their battle skills, magical weapons, and armor are unmatched by anyone. Elves are also very loyal and will always come to the aid of those they consider friends.

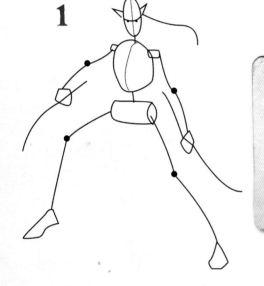

1

SIZE: 6 TO 6.5 FEET (1.8 TO 2 M) TALL

HABITAT: FORESTS AND PEACEFUL MOUNTAIN VALLEYS

Physical Features: Elves look slender and delicate, yet they are quite strong and athletic. They're usually considered very attractive and have long, straight hair. But elves are best known for their pointed ears, bright eyes, and smiling faces.

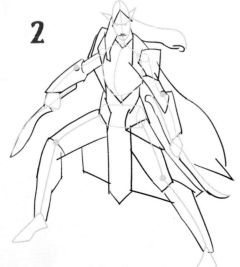

2

3

FINAL

6

WHAT'S NEXT?

After practicing this elf,
try drawing him tracking
an orc raiding party
through the forest.

4

5

49

DARK ELVES

Dark elves live in a dangerous and violent world. Strong families of dark elves often battle one another for control over their underground cities. Whether using swords or powerful magic spells, most dark elves enjoy attacking and killing their enemies. They often raid cities and villages to steal food, supplies, and people to work as slaves.

SIZE: ABOUT 5.5 TO 6 FEET (1.7 TO 1.8 M) TALL

HABITAT: LARGE CITIES DEEP UNDER THE EARTH

Physical Features: Dark elves have slender bodies, pointed ears, and are usually very good-looking. They are known for their very dark skin and straight white hair. Most dark elves have red or yellow eyes. But in rare cases, a dark elf may have dark blue or purple eyes.

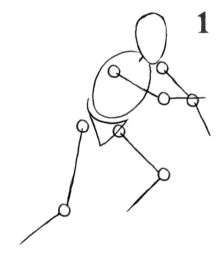

1

2

3

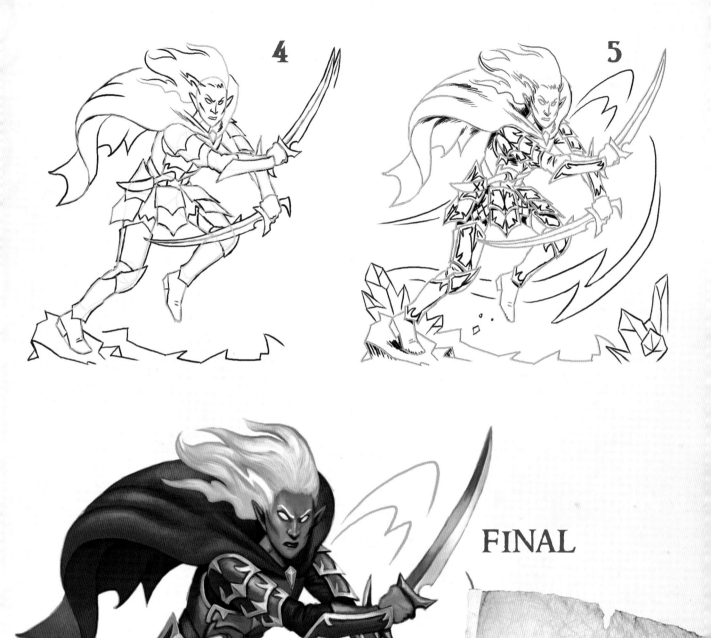

4

5

FINAL

WHAT'S NEXT?

When you feel comfortable drawing this dark elf, try showing another one fighting a giant spider or other underground monster.

MERFOLK

Merfolk don't like intruders and fiercely protect their territories. If they see ships in their waters, merfolk will at first smile and motion for the sailors to follow them. But the merfolk's friendliness is just a trick used to lead ships away from their hidden cities. Once at a safe distance, they simply disappear and swim away under the water.

SIZE: ABOUT 7 FEET (2.1 M) LONG

HABITAT: SHALLOW SEAS NEAR TROPICAL COASTS; SOME DEEP INLAND LAKES

Physical Features: Merfolk appear similar to humans from the waist up. They have fair skin, athletic bodies, and waist-length hair. Their lower bodies are like large scaly fish. Their tails end in large fins or flippers used for quickly swimming through the water.

3

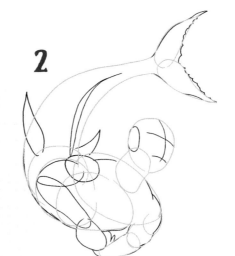

1

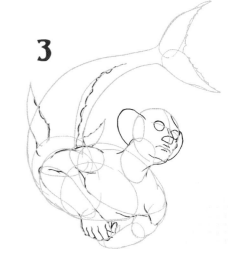

2

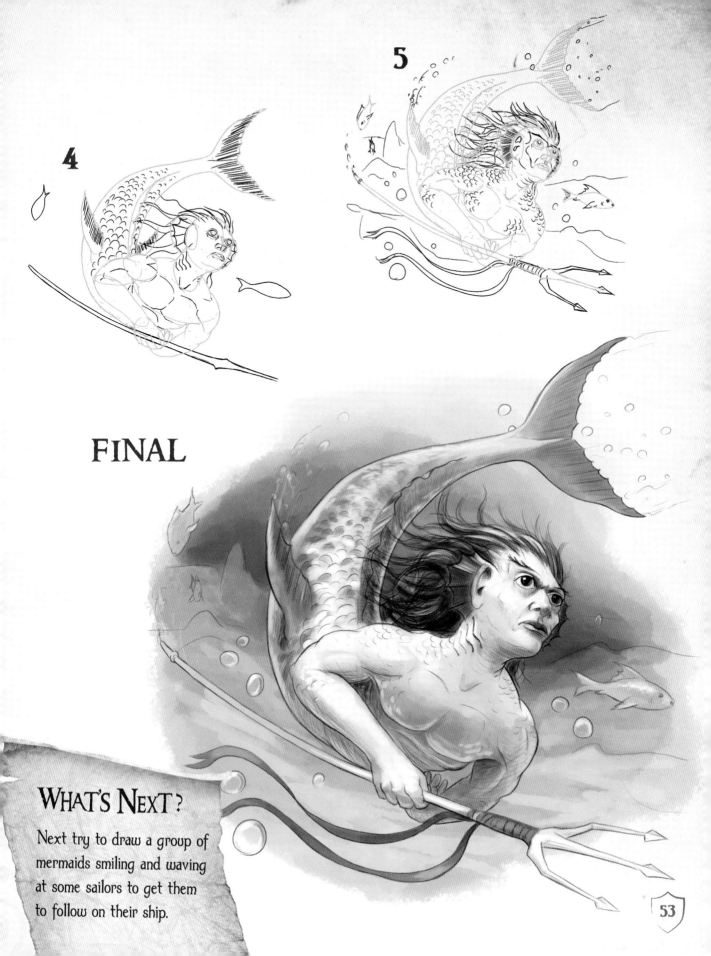

4

5

FINAL

WHAT'S NEXT?

Next try to draw a group of
mermaids smiling and waving
at some sailors to get them
to follow on their ship.

TREEFOLK

Treefolk are the guardians of the forest. They spend their days protecting trees from being cut down. Treefolk are extremely slow in almost everything they do. However, if they become angry, treefolk can be fearsome. They can easily tear down a large stone fortress in less than a day.

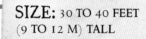

SIZE: 30 TO 40 FEET (9 TO 12 M) TALL

HABITAT: THICK FORESTS WITH MANY TREES

Physical Features: Treefolk look very much like trees. They have thick, trunklike legs, and their feet look like tree roots. Their arms and hands look like tree branches, and their skin is similar to thick, rough bark. Treefolk usually have large, crooked noses, and some grow beards made of thick vines or moss.

1

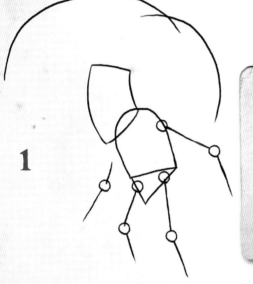

2

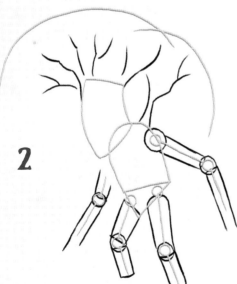

3

WHAT'S NEXT?

Next try drawing a group of different types of treefolk as they gather to meet by a stream or in a forest meadow.

FINAL

4

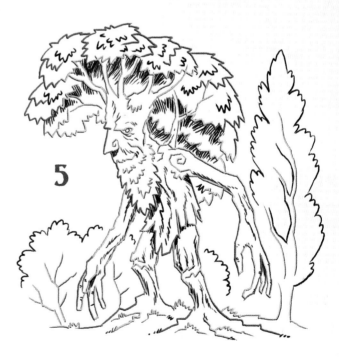

5

ELVES vs. ORCS

In a time before anyone can remember, elves and orcs may have been distantly related. Both races may have shared interests and physical qualities. But at some point in the past, orcs became corrupt and evil. They became greedy and obsessed with gold and treasures. Over time they grew violent and began killing others, and each other, to get the treasure they craved. They also became hateful of their peaceful elf cousins. Orcs and elves have been mortal enemies ever since. Whenever they meet, they attack each other on sight.

ELVES

SIZE: 6 TO 6.5 FEET
(1.8 TO 2 M) TALL

HABITAT: FORESTS AND
PEACEFUL MOUNTAIN VALLEYS

ORCS

SIZE: 4.5 TO 5 FEET
(1.4 TO 1.5 M) TALL

HABITAT: DARK
MOUNTAIN CAVES OR
RUINED CASTLES OR FORTS

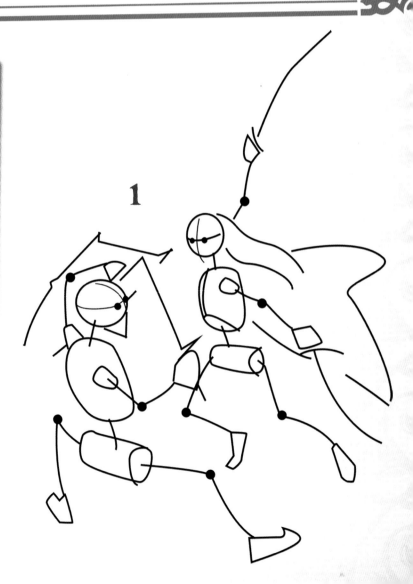

1

2

3

4

5

WHAT'S NEXT?

After practicing this drawing, try to create a large and fierce battle scene. Draw several elves and orcs fighting on a mountainside. Try drawing them in various fighting poses and with different types of weapons.

FINAL

GRIFFINS

Griffins usually live alone and spend much of their time hunting for food. They can track prey over long distances. Occasionally they will hunt in small packs to trap and kill large prey. A few griffins are friendly toward people and may offer help to those in need.

SIZE: 7 TO 7.5 FEET (2.1 TO 2.3 M) LONG; WINGSPAN UP TO 20 FEET (6 M)

HABITAT: DRY CAVES IN GRASSY HILLS OR MOUNTAIN REGIONS

Physical Features: A griffin's upper body has the head, wings, and razor-sharp talons of a large bird of prey. Its lower body features the powerful legs, claws, and tail of a lion. Griffins are usually covered with a mix of golden hair and feathers. They also have incredible eyesight and can spot a rabbit moving up to 3 miles (5 kilometers) away.

1

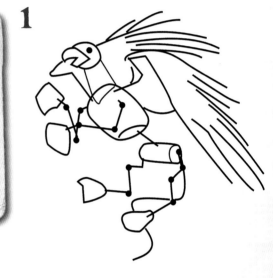

2

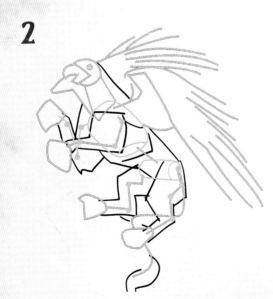

3

FINAL

WHAT'S NEXT?

After drawing this griffin, try drawing it flying into battle to help its human friends.

4

5

HARPIES

Harpies are often found perched on rocky cliffs by the sea watching for prey. Harpies will eat almost any kind of meat, but they like human flesh the best. They use their magical singing ability to cloud the minds of human victims and draw them close before attacking. Harpies never bother to bathe themselves. They stink horribly from the bits of rotting filth that cover their feathered bodies.

SIZE: 4 TO 4.5 FEET (1.2 TO 1.4 M) TALL; WINGSPAN UP TO 9 FEET (2.7 M)

HABITAT: ROCKY CLIFFS AND SMALL CAVES NEAR THE SEA

Physical Features: Harpies have the bodies of large birds such as vultures or owls. They have large, powerful wings and strong scaly legs. Their feet are tipped with razor-sharp talons. However, harpies' heads appear as hideous women with yellow eyes, greasy hair, and decaying teeth.

1

2

3

WHAT'S NEXT?

Next try to draw a small flock of harpies perched on a cliff trying to lure a ship of sailors closer to shore with their magical singing.

FINAL

4

5

PHOENIXES

Phoenixes are very private creatures. They prefer to live far from humans. But these mysterious birds are good and noble. They do whatever they can to fight the forces of evil. In rare cases phoenixes have become loyal friends to good wizards. They come to their friends' aid whenever they are called.

SIZE: 10 TO 12 FEET (3 TO 3.7 M) TALL; WINGSPAN UP TO 30 FEET (9 M)

HABITAT: ROCKY CLIFFS IN MOUNTAIN REGIONS

Physical Features: When a phoenix becomes angry, its feathers begin to glow a fiery red color. These powerful magical birds are strong enough to lift and carry an adult elephant. Phoenix tears can magically heal serious wounds in a matter of seconds. Phoenix feathers also have magical properties. Wizards often place them inside their magic wands to make them more powerful.

1

2

3

4

5

WHAT'S NEXT?

Now try drawing this phoenix fighting alongside its wizard friend as they battle an army of wicked orcs and goblins.

FINAL

PEGASI

Pegasi live alone in the wild and are not easily tamed. They are intelligent and do not tolerate evil. They react violently toward wicked people. However, if someone treats a pegasus with respect, it may become a loyal friend. It may even allow that person to ride it into battle.

SIZE: 8 TO 8.5 FEET (2.4 TO 2.6 M) LONG; WINGSPAN UP TO 25 FEET (7.6 M)

HABITAT: FORESTS AND GRASSY PLAINS

Physical Features: Pegasi are very similar to horses. They have powerful bodies, strong legs, muscular necks, and noble faces. Their hair is usually white or light gray. Their powerful wings allow them to fly up to 50 miles (80 km) per hour. Their manes and tails are made of hair and feathers.

1

2

3

WHAT'S NEXT?

After drawing this pegasus, try to draw it flying into battle carrying a human warrior on its back.

FINAL

4

5

UNICORNS

Unicorns are fierce protectors of their forest homes. They do not tolerate evil in any form. They normally live alone or with a mate deep in the forest. Unicorns want nothing to do with humans. But they are often friendly toward elves and other creatures that respect nature.

SIZE: 8 TO 8.5 FEET (2.4 TO 2.6 M) LONG

HABITAT: GRASSY CLEARINGS IN LARGE FORESTS

Physical Features: Unicorns resemble large white horses. However, they usually have bright blue or violet eyes. A unicorn's most famous feature is the 2 to 3 foot (0.6 to 0.9 m) ivory horn that grows from its head. These horns have strong magical properties. They can be used to make strong healing potions. Some wizards even craft unicorn horns into powerful magic wands.

1

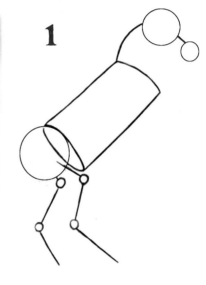

2

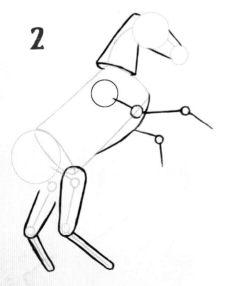

3

4

5

FINAL

WHAT'S NEXT?

When you're done drawing this unicorn, try drawing two of them chasing a wicked forest troll out of the woods.

MINOTAURS

Minotaurs spend most of their time prowling their mazelike caves for their next meal. They have an amazing sense of direction and never get lost. This ability is a great advantage. It helps minotaurs hunt down humans and other prey that wander into their mazelike homes.

SIZE: 7.5 TO 8 FEET (2.3 TO 2.4 M) TALL

HABITAT: MAZELIKE NETWORKS OF UNDERGROUND CAVES OR TUNNELS AND SEWERS UNDER ANCIENT CITIES

Physical Features: Minotaurs are a strange combination of humans and bulls. Their heads and lower bodies are like a bull's. But their arms and torsos are similar to a human's. Minotaurs are covered in shaggy black or brown hair and have hooves instead of feet. All minotaurs have sharp, deadly horns used for attacking their enemies and prey.

1

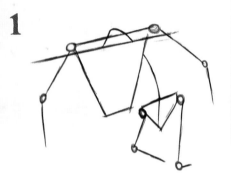

2

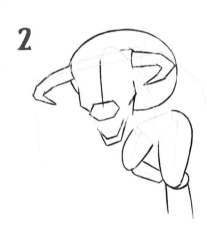

3

4

5

FINAL

WHAT'S NEXT?

After drawing this fierce minotaur, try drawing it chasing down its next victim in its mazelike cave.

CHIMERAS

Most chimeras are dim-witted beasts. They normally live alone and spend much of their time hunting for food. These creatures are completely loyal to the wicked gods and wizards who created them. If a chimera's creator orders it to attack an enemy, it will do so without question.

SIZE: 6.5 FEET (2 M) TALL; 15 FEET (4.6 M) LONG
HABITAT: DRY CAVES IN HILLY REGIONS

Physical Features: Chimeras are a combination of several creatures. Most have two heads—one of a powerful lion and one of a horned goat. A chimera's tail takes the form of a huge snake with a deadly, poisonous bite. These beasts have front feet resembling a dragon's claws and their hind feet are shaped like a goat's hooves.

1

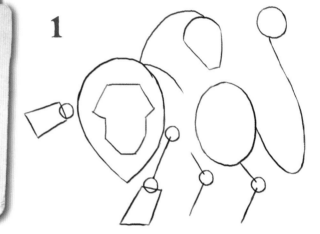

2

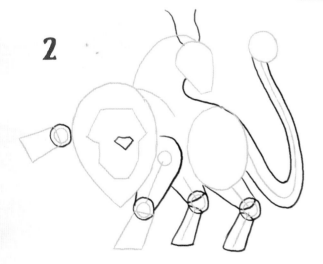

3

4

5

FINAL

WHAT'S NEXT?

After practicing this chimera, try drawing one with different kinds of heads. Give it a tiger's head, a bear's head, or even the head and wings of a dragon!

GORGONS

Gorgons prefer to live by themselves and don't like intruders. Most gorgons are expert shots with bows and arrows. They also have a powerful magical defense. One look from an angry gorgon's glowing eyes will turn an enemy to stone. Gorgon lairs are often filled with statues of those foolish enough to be caught by these wicked creatures.

SIZE: 5 TO 5.5 FEET (1.5 TO 1.7 M) TALL

HABITAT: CAVES AND OLD CASTLES NEAR THE SEA

Physical Features: Most gorgons have lower bodies resembling large snakes. They have rough, scaly skin that is usually green or brown in color. They have jagged teeth, sharp fangs, and a forked tongue. Gorgons are most famous for the nest of squirming snakes they have in place of normal hair.

1

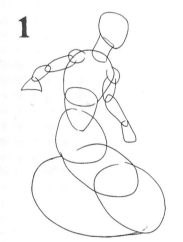

2

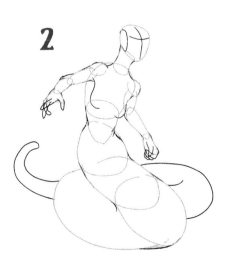

3

4

5

6

FINAL

WHAT'S NEXT?

Now try drawing another gorgon as she hunts for a new victim inside her ruined castle by the sea.

CERBERUS

Cerberus spends its time wandering rocky plains and lava fields near volcanoes. Nobody knows why it lurks in such locations. It's thought that Cerberus may be guarding a secret entrance to its master's lair. An evil wizard may have raised Cerberus up from the Underworld to be his personal guard dog.

SIZE: 6.5 TO 7 FEET (2 TO 2.1 M) TALL

HABITAT: ROCKY PLAINS AND LAVA FIELDS

Physical Features: Cerberus appears as a huge, three-headed dog. It's covered with short brown and black hair. The beast's feet are tipped with sharp claws, and each of its three mouths is filled with wicked, gnashing teeth. Cerberus can launch large balls of fire from its mouths to overwhelm its victims.

1

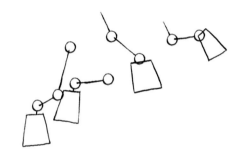

2

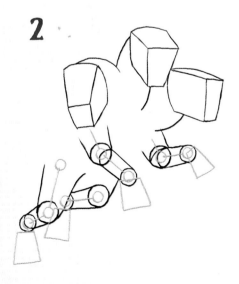

3

4

5

FINAL

WHAT'S NEXT?

Next try drawing
Cerberus belching out a
huge fireball at a victim
near its volcano home.

77

SEA SERPENTS

Sea serpents spend almost all of their time hunting for food. These creatures normally hunt large prey like whales or giant squid. But they will occasionally attack human ships. They first coil their huge bodies around the ships and crush them. They then eat the sailors who try to jump to safety. Only a few sailors have survived a sea serpent's attack.

SIZE: 150 TO 200 FEET (46 TO 61 M) LONG

HABITAT: WARM OCEAN WATERS

Physical Features: Sea serpents are often called sea dragons because of their dragonlike appearance. Their gigantic snakelike bodies are covered with tough scaly skin. Many sea serpents have dragonlike heads and mouths filled with deadly teeth. Some sea serpents may even have large fins that resemble a dragon's wings.

1

2

3

5

4

6

FINAL

WHAT'S NEXT?

After practicing this drawing, try showing the sea serpent in a major battle against a giant squid.

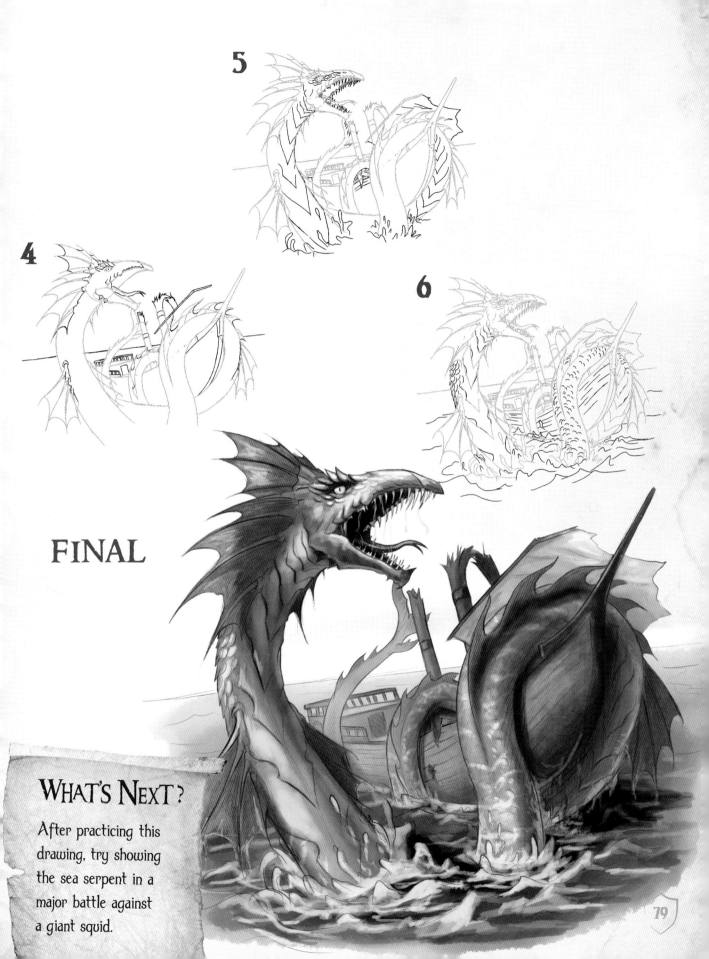

KRAKENS

Krakens are among the largest and deadliest creatures of any fantasy world. They like attacking ships and enjoy the taste of human flesh. A kraken first wraps its huge tentacles around a ship. It then crushes the ship and pulls it under the water. After sinking the ship, the monster grabs the doomed sailors and stuffs them into its gaping mouth.

SIZE: MORE THAN 350 FEET (107 M) LONG
HABITAT: LARGE CAVES ON THE OCEAN FLOOR

Physical Features: Krakens resemble gigantic squids or octopuses with tough, rubbery skin. Their huge eyes help them find prey in the darkest ocean waters. Krakens are best known for their 10 powerful tentacles. However, their deadly mouths are filled with hundreds of huge, swordlike teeth that can kill prey in an instant.

1

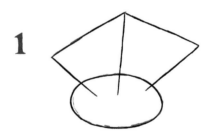

2

3

FINAL

4

6

5

WHAT'S NEXT?

When you're done drawing this huge kraken, try a new drawing that shows it attacking a large merchant ship.

CHIMERA vs. CERBERUS

Long ago two evil wizards desired to control the same country. To gain an advantage, one of them created the vicious chimera. He used it to force local villagers to obey his will. Not to be outdone, the second wizard raised Cerberus from the Underworld to even the odds. The two mythical beasts are evenly matched in fierceness and strength. They are locked in a never-ending battle, and nobody can say which one will claim the ultimate victory for its master.

CHIMERA

SIZE: ABOUT 6.5 FEET (2 M) TALL; UP TO 15 FEET (4.6 M) LONG

HABITAT: DRY CAVES IN HILLY REGIONS

CERBERUS

SIZE: 6.5 TO 7 FEET (2 TO 2.1 M) TALL

HABITAT: ROCKY PLAINS AND LAVA FIELDS

1

2

3

4

5

6

7

8

9

WHAT'S NEXT?

When you're finished with this drawing, try adding more mythical beasts to the battle. Do you think the minotaur would fight with the chimera? Will a gorgon join up with Cerberus? The choice is up to you!

FINAL

PIXIES

Pixies love to play tricks and practical jokes on people. But their pranks often go too far and result in damage or injuries to others. For this reason, many people feel that pixies are nasty and wicked pests. Pixies also enjoy stealing small items such as thimbles, toothpicks, and pieces of wire. Their small homes are often filled with the worthless trinkets they've stolen from others.

SIZE: 6 TO 8 INCHES (15 TO 20 CM) TALL

HABITAT: HOLLOW TREES, LOGS, AND SIMILAR SPACES IN WOODED AREAS

Physical Features: At first glance it's easy to mistake pixies for fairies. They have large eyes, pointed ears, and butterfly-like wings. However, their clothing is often made from dead leaves and grass or bits of dark cloth they've stolen from others.

1

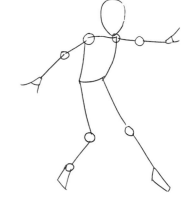

2

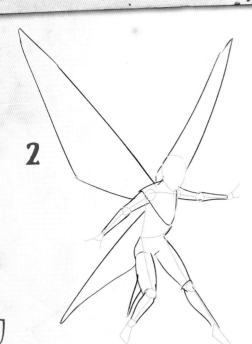

3

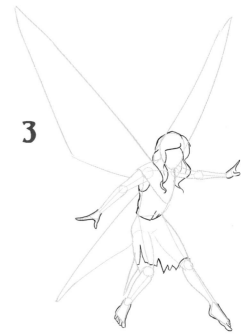

4

5

FINAL

6

WHAT'S NEXT?

After drawing this little pixie, try drawing a group of them as they play a nasty prank on a dwarf in the forest.

87

NIXIES

Nixies are fiercely private. They are usually peaceful, but some can be violent. They are willing to drive away intruders by force. A few nixies have an even more wicked nature. They enjoy using their magical abilities to trap innocent people and use them as slaves.

SIZE: 4 TO 4.5 FEET (1.2 TO 1.4 M) TALL

HABITAT: WARM FRESHWATER PONDS AND LAKES

Physical Features: Nixies strongly resemble beautiful mermaids. However, instead of fishlike tails, nixies have two froglike legs and flippers for feet. Their pale green skin is made of tiny fishlike scales. Instead of ears, nixies have gills that allow them to breathe underwater. Most nixies also have dark green hair that resembles seaweed.

1

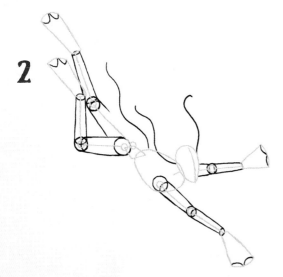

2

3

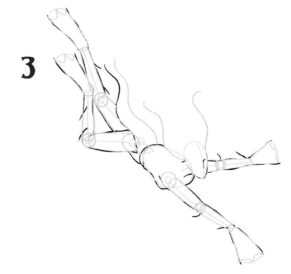

4

5

FINAL

WHAT'S NEXT?

Next try to draw a small group of nixies chasing away an intruder from their territory.

SIRENS

Sirens are fierce and hungry hunters. When they spot unwary sailors, they use magical singing and illusions to cloud the sailors' minds. The sailors believe the creatures are beautiful women calling to them from shore. The dazed sailors usually end up smashing their ships on nearby rocks. The sirens can then easily capture their helpless prey.

SIZE: 6 TO 6.5 FEET (1.8 TO 2 M) LONG

HABITAT: ROCKY ISLANDS AND SHORELINES NEAR THE SEA

Physical Features: In their true form, sirens look like monstrous mermaids. They have scaly blue or green skin. Their webbed hands are tipped with wicked claws, and their mouths are filled with sharp, needlelike teeth. Sirens also have a strong tail that helps them swim quickly.

1

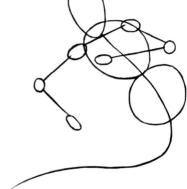

2

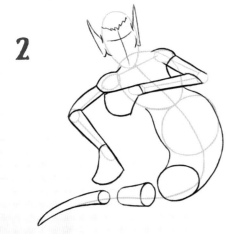

3

4

5

6

FINAL

WHAT'S NEXT?

Now try drawing a group of sirens trying to trick sailors into moving their ship closer to a dangerous rocky shore.

HAGS

Hags are completely evil. Their powerful evil often causes disease and decay where they live. Green forests soon die and wetlands become stinking, rotten swamps. Hags have a strong hunger for human flesh. They often disguise themselves with magic to lure people into their lairs. Once a hag traps a victim, she enjoys taking her time to satisfy her unnatural hunger.

SIZE: 5.5 TO 6 FEET (1.7 TO 1.8 M) TALL

HABITAT: DAMP CAVES OR RUN-DOWN SHACKS IN DARK FORESTS OR SWAMPS

Physical Features: Hags are known for their hideous appearance. They have shriveled bodies, hunched backs, and mouths full of black, rotting teeth. Their skin is usually covered with warts and open sores. Hags also have bony arms and long fingers tipped with sharp black claws.

1

2

3

4

5

6

FINAL

WHAT'S NEXT?

After practicing this hag, try drawing her next to a large kettle and a fire as she prepares to cook her next victim!

BOGGARTS

Boggarts are wicked creatures who love to cause trouble. They enjoy breaking or stealing eyeglasses, keys, and other important items. Boggarts never kill, but they don't mind hurting people. One of their favorite tricks is to scatter tacks on the floor next to people's beds. The wicked creatures then wake their victims with a loud noise. They watch with glee as people stumble out of bed and step on the sharp objects.

SIZE: 8 TO 12 INCHES (20 TO 30 CM) TALL

HABITAT: BROOM CLOSETS, ATTICS, AND SIMILAR SPACES IN OLD HOUSES

Physical Features: Boggarts are brownies that have become very angry and have changed into a monstrous form. They have beady black or red eyes, long pointed ears, and coarse whiskers. Their snarling mouths are filled with nasty sharp teeth.

1

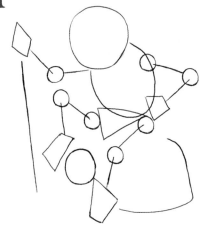

2

3

4

5

FINAL

WHAT'S NEXT?

Next try drawing this boggart watching and laughing at a sleepy victim stepping on sharp tacks scattered on the floor.

95

GREMLINS

Gremlins are nasty creatures that delight in causing trouble. They care nothing about the safety of others or even each other. In fact, they especially enjoy it when someone is injured or killed from their mischievous deeds. Sunlight is deadly to gremlins, so they live deep underground. They come to the surface only on the darkest of nights.

SIZE: 2 TO 2.5 FEET (0.6 TO 0.8 M) TALL

HABITAT: DEEP, DARK, UNDERGROUND CAVES

Physical Features: Gremlins have tough, scaly skin that is usually green or brown. Their large glowing eyes are usually green or red. Gremlins have mouths filled with jagged teeth, and their long fingers are tipped with sharp claws. Gremlins also have huge ears shaped like a bat's wings.

1

2

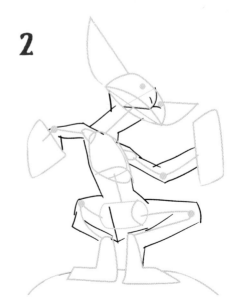

3

4

5

FINAL

WHAT'S NEXT?

After drawing this
mischievous gremlin,
try drawing an army
of them causing chaos in
a small village at night.

97

GOBLINS

Goblins don't produce food or useful goods of their own. They instead raid nearby farms or villages at night to steal what they need. However, goblins are clever at making simple weapons and traps to protect their underground homes.

SIZE: 4 TO 4.5 FEET (1.2 TO 1.4 M) TALL
HABITAT: DARK MOUNTAIN TUNNELS AND CAVES

Physical Features: Goblins look similar to orcs and are often mistaken for them. However, goblins are shorter and smaller. They also stand and walk in a bent-over posture. Goblins have large pointed ears and mouths full of sharp, jagged teeth. They have very large yellow or green eyes, which help them see in the dark. Bright light is painful for goblins. They hate the sun and never leave their dark caves during the day.

1

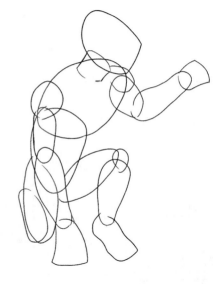

2

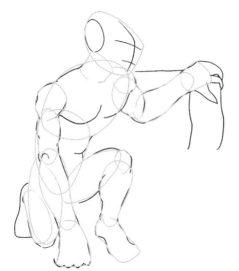

3

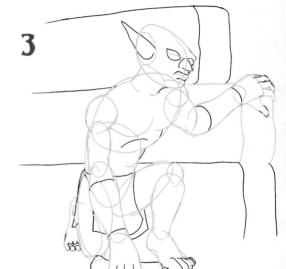

4

5

FINAL

WHAT'S NEXT?

When you've finished this
goblin, try drawing several
more fighting over a shiny
silver necklace or golden cup.

99

HOBGOBLINS

Hobgoblins live a military lifestyle. Their young begin training to fight as soon as they can hold a weapon. Hobgoblins are skilled at creating and using complex weapons such as catapults and crossbows. They are also tireless fighters. During battle they keep fighting until they either win or are killed.

SIZE: 5.5 TO 6 FEET (1.7 TO 1.8 M) TALL

HABITAT: DARK MOUNTAIN CAVES OR THE RUINS OF STONE CASTLES OR FORTS

Physical Features: Hobgoblins are related to goblins and orcs but have some different features. Their muscular bodies are covered in coarse brown or black hair. Their eyes are usually yellow or red. Hobgoblins also have two large tusks jutting up from their lower jaws. Many hobgoblins like to weave bits of bone or metal trinkets into their long hair and beards.

1

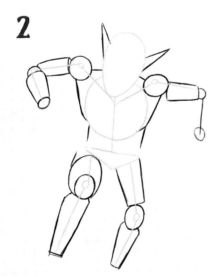

2

3

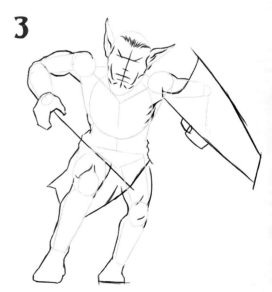

4

5

FINAL

WHAT'S NEXT?

Next try to draw a scene showing a hobgoblin raiding party attacking a dwarf mountain stronghold.

ORCS

Most orcs aren't very intelligent. However, they can be clever craftsmen. They often make ugly yet effective weapons and armor from simple materials. Orcs are cruel and violent creatures with short tempers. They often fight violently with each other over small disagreements. They also enjoy attacking and burning entire villages to the ground.

SIZE: 4.5 TO 5 FEET (1.4 TO 1.5 M) TALL

HABITAT: DARK MOUNTAIN CAVES OR RUINED CASTLES OR FORTS

Physical Features: Orcs have a wide variety of appearances. They can have black, gray, green, red-brown, or pale white skin. They may have long, greasy hair, or no hair at all. Nearly all orcs have ugly, deformed faces with yellow eyes, pointed ears, and crooked mouths full of jagged teeth. Many orcs are covered in nasty scars left from combat wounds.

1

2

3

4

WHAT'S NEXT?

After drawing this scary orc, try drawing a pack of them chasing after a group of travelers through an old overgrown forest.

FINAL

5

BLACK ORCS

Black orcs are violent, cruel, and have short tempers. They don't care about others and will kill anyone who dares to insult them. Black orcs are highly skilled warriors. From their first breath, they are taught how to fight. They often use clever battle plans and complex weapons to attack enemies. Given enough time, an army of black orcs can defeat even the best defended fortress.

SIZE: 6.5 TO 7 FEET (2 TO 2.1 M) TALL

HABITAT: MOUNTAIN CAVES OR STRONG FORTS CONTROLLED BY EVIL WIZARDS OR WARLORDS

Physical Features: Black orcs have strong, muscular bodies. Their black skin is thick and tough, which is often marked by large scars from battle. Black orcs have yellow eyes, pointed ears, and greasy black hair. Their snarling mouths are filled with sharp, jagged teeth.

1

2

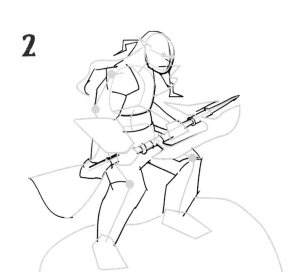

3

4

5

FINAL

WHAT'S NEXT?

Next try to draw an army of black orcs as they fight a huge battle near the strong walls of a stone fortress.

TROGLODYTES

Troglodytes are almost always hungry for meat and treasure. They are also strong and fierce fighters. Troglodytes often raid nearby settlements to steal food, weapons, treasure—and people. They use captured villagers as slaves, food, or sacrifices to their evil gods.

SIZE: 5 TO 5.5 FEET (1.5 TO 1.7 M) TALL
HABITAT: WET UNDERGROUND CAVES OR DARK SWAMPY REGIONS

Physical Features: Troglodytes have muscular bodies with scaly green or blue-green skin. Their lizardlike eyes are usually green or yellow and help them see well in the dark. Troglodytes have very strong jaws and mouths filled with razor-sharp teeth. They also have long, powerful tails similar to alligator tails. Male troglodytes have colorful frills that run from their heads to their tails.

1

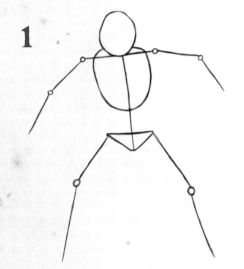

2

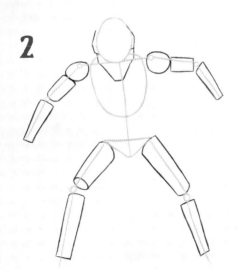

3

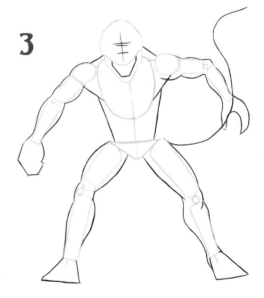

4

5

FINAL

WHAT'S NEXT?

Now try drawing some troglodytes leading their human prisoners back to their swampy lair.

GOBLIN NIGHT RAID

Late one night a sleepy mountain village lies under the light of a full moon. Suddenly, the silence is shattered by the sound of a horn piercing the air. Before long the streets are filled with torchlight and the coarse shrieks of a goblin raiding party. The wicked creatures have come to steal food, weapons, and other goods. Many of the goblins won't survive the night. But before the night is done, the nasty creatures will destroy several buildings and steal as many supplies as they can carry.

GOBLINS

SIZE: 4 TO 4.5 FEET (1.2 TO 1.4 M) TALL

HABITAT: DARK MOUNTAIN TUNNELS AND CAVES

VILLAGERS

SIZE: 5 TO 6 FEET (1.5 TO 1.8 M) TALL

HOMES: PEACEFUL FARMS, VILLAGES, AND OTHER SETTLEMENTS

1

2

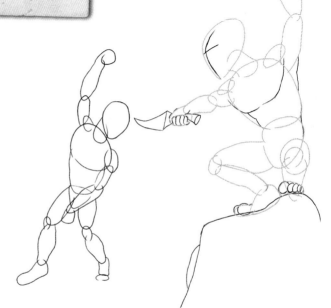

3

4

5

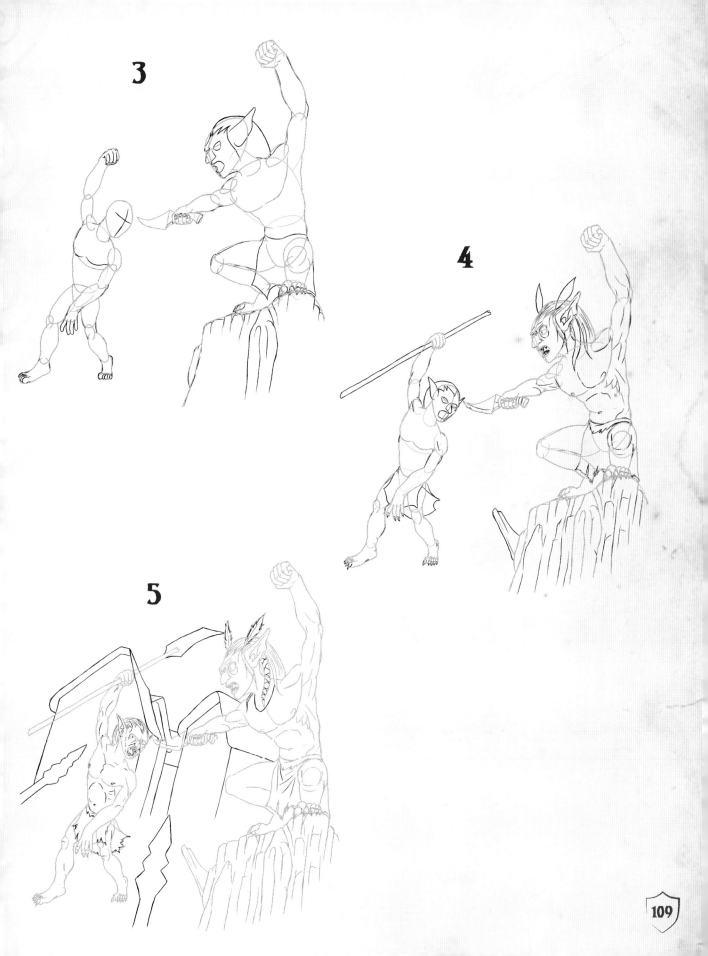

6

7

8

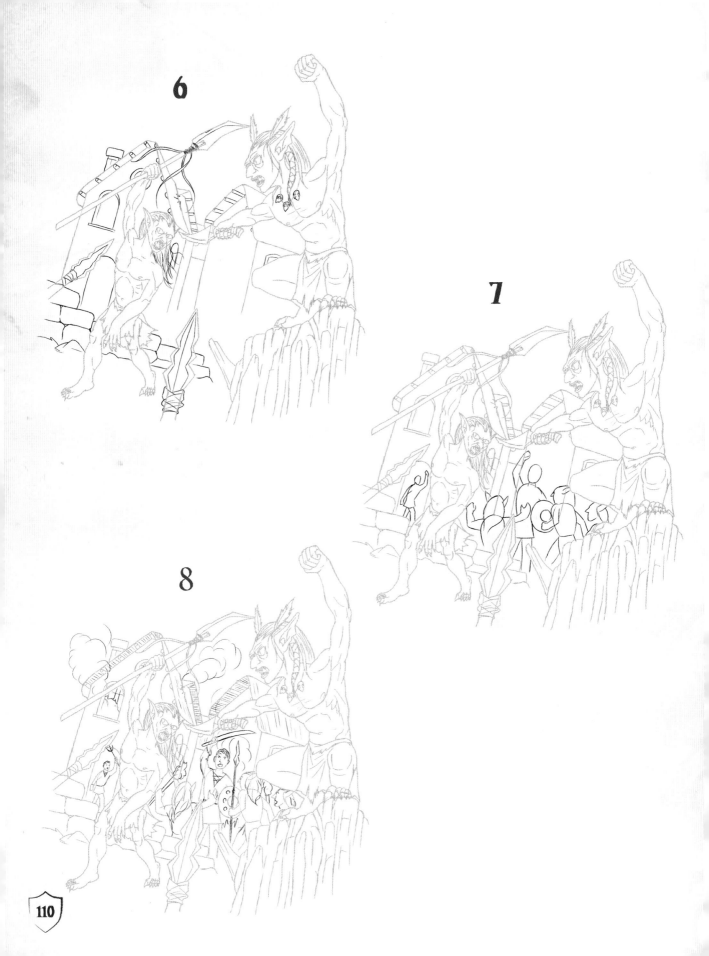

WHAT'S NEXT?

When you've finished this drawing, try another scene showing a different part of the village. Try drawing the goblins sneaking past the village guards or fighting villagers in the center of town.

FINAL

Capstone Press is published by Capstone
1710 Roe Crest Drive, Mankato, Minnesota 56003
www.mycapstone.com

Library of Congress Cataloging-in-Publication Data
Names: Sautter, Aaron, author. | Bustamante, Martin (Illustrator), illustrator.
Title: Drawing fantasy creatures / by A.J. Sautter; illustrated by Martin
Bustamante, Stefano Azzalin, Tom McGrath, Jason Juta, Colin Howard.
Description: North Mankato, MN : Capstone Press, 2017. |
Description based on print version record and CIP data provided by publisher;
resource not viewed.
Identifiers: LCCN 2016001332 (print) | LCCN 2016000616 (ebook) |
ISBN 9781491486719 (eBook PDF) | ISBN 9781491486702 (paperback)
Subjects: LCSH: Art and mythology—Juvenile literature. | Animals, Mythical,
in art—Juvenile literature. | Drawing—Technique—Juvenile literature.
Classification: LCC NC825.M9 (print) | LCC NC825.M9 S28 2017 (ebook) |
DDC 743/.87—dc23
LC record available at http://lccn.loc.gov/2016001332

Summary: Simple, step-by-step instructions teach readers how to draw a wide
variety of fantasy creatures, including background information about each.

Editorial Credits:
Designers: Kyle Grenz and Tracy McCabe
Media Researcher: Kelly Garvin
Production Specialist: Laura Manthe

Image Credits: Capstone Press: Collin Howard, cover, 1, 12–13, 14–15, 34–35,
40–41, 42–43, 68–69, 70–71, 80–81, 90–91, 100–101, 106–107, Jason Juta, cover,
backcover, 1, 4, 5 (top)(bottom right), 10–11, 18–19, 26–27, 28–29, 50–51, 54–55,
72–73, 76–77, 82–85, 88–89, 94–95, Martin Bustamante, cover, backcover, 1, 6 (top
right), 16–17, 20–21, 48–49, 56–59, 60–61, 62–63, 64–65, 66–67, 96–97, 102–103,
104–105, Stefano Azzalin, cover, backcover, 1, 5, 22–23, 24–25, 36–37, 38–39,
44–45, 52–53, 74–75, 78–79, 98–99, 108–111, Tom McGrath, cover, backcover, 1, 5
(left), 8–9, 30–33, 46–47, 86–87, 92–93

Artistic Elements: Shutterstock: aopsan, Bambuh, blue pencil, Kompaniets
Taras, Marta Jonina, Molodec, val lawless

The author dedicates this book to the writers and artists who
inspire people to dream of fantastic worlds, creatures, and adventures
far more interesting than our own. — A.J. Sautter

Printed in China.
042017   010388R